A Little Extra Money

Paulette Durand

Paulette Durand

Copyright Page

First edition

Index

Extra Money?

Two words that sound pretty good, right? Imagine that after paying all your bills and regular expenses, you still have some money left over to enjoy. Maybe you want to save up for a trip, pay off debt faster, or just have a cushion for emergencies. Earning extra money while you have a regular job may seem difficult, but it's more doable than you think. The first thing you need to understand is that there are many ways to do it, and not all of them require huge sacrifices of time or effort. The key is to find something you're passionate about and that fits your lifestyle.

First, think about your skills and hobbies. Do you have any special talents that you could monetize? Maybe you're good with your hands and enjoy woodworking, or perhaps you're a master in the kitchen and could sell your delicious cakes. There are people who make extra money simply by sharing what they love to do. For example, if you love photography, you could offer photo shoots on the weekends. If you love writing, you could start a blog and eventually monetize it with advertising or affiliate marketing. The idea is to turn what you already enjoy into a source of income.

Another popular option is freelancing. Platforms like Upwork or Fiverr allow you to offer your services to a global audience. If you have skills in graphic design, programming, writing, or translation, you can find clients who need exactly what you offer. The great thing about freelancing is that you can do it in your spare time, fitting it into your schedule. You could even turn it into a small business if you see that it's successful. Plus, working this way allows you to build a portfolio and gain experience, which is beneficial for your main career.

You can also consider selling products online. Platforms like Etsy, eBay, or Amazon are great places to start. If you have a knack for creating things, such as jewelry, custom clothing, or art, you could open an online store and sell your products. You don't need a huge initial investment; many times, you can start with materials you already have at home. As your business grows, you could reinvest your profits to expand your offering. You could even buy products wholesale and resell them at a higher price. The important thing is to find a niche that you're passionate about and where you see a demand.

Another way to make extra money is by offering your knowledge and skills as a tutor or instructor. If you are good at math, science, languages, or any other subject, you could tutor students. You could also create online courses on topics you are good at and sell them on platforms like Udemy or Teachable. Online education is a growing field, and there are always people looking to learn new skills. Not only does this allow you to make extra money, but it also allows you to help others achieve their educational goals.

If you prefer something more flexible, you could join the gig economy. Driving for Uber or Lyft in your spare time, renting out a room in your home through Airbnb, or running errands for others with apps like TaskRabbit are all effective ways to earn extra money without compromising your main job. These platforms allow you to work whenever you want, which is ideal if you have an irregular schedule. Plus, you can meet new people and have interesting experiences while you work.

Finally, don't forget about investments. While it may sound intimidating, investing in stocks, bonds, or real estate can be a great way to generate passive income. Start with small amounts and learn as you go. There are plenty of apps and platforms that make investing accessible to everyone, even if you don't have a lot of money to start with. Over time, your investments can grow and provide you with a stable source of additional income.

Earning extra money doesn't have to be a daunting task. It's about finding what works for you, something you enjoy and can do without sacrificing your well-being. With a little creativity and effort, you can discover ways to increase your income and reach your financial goals. Remember that every little effort counts and every step you take brings you closer to financial freedom. So start exploring your options today and find a way to earn that extra money you so desire.

Knowing Yourself

This is the first and perhaps most important step when it comes to making extra money. Why? Because when you understand who you are, what your skills are, and what you are passionate about, you can find ways to make money that are not only effective, but rewarding as well. Imagine doing something you really love and getting paid for it. Sounds ideal, right? Well, to get to that point, you first need to do some honest, deep introspection.

Start by thinking about what you really enjoy doing. What are those activities that make you lose track of time? Maybe you enjoy gardening, painting, writing stories, or cooking. Jot down all of these activities, no matter how trivial they may seem. This is your starting point. Then, ask yourself which of these activities you could turn into a source of income. For example, if you love to cook, you might consider selling home-cooked meals, offering cooking classes, or even starting a recipe blog.

Next, assess your skills. Not just the skills you use in your current job, but also those you've developed throughout your life. Are you good at listening to others and giving advice? Maybe you could offer coaching or counseling services. Do you have a knack for organization and planning? You could help others organize their events or even their lives. Make a list of all your skills and then think about how you could use them to make extra money.

Now, consider your personality. Are you an outgoing person who enjoys interacting with others, or do you prefer to work in solitude? This is important because not all opportunities to earn extra money are suitable for everyone. If you are a people person, you might enjoy working as a tour guide, organizing events, or even selling products at fairs and markets. On the other hand, if you prefer quiet time, perhaps working online as a freelance writer, graphic designer, or programmer is more suitable for you.

Once you're clear on what you like to do, what you're good at, and what type of work suits your personality, it's time to do some research. Search the internet and your community for opportunities that align with your interests and skills. Read stories from people who have managed to make extra money in ways similar to the ones you're considering. Not only will this give you ideas, but it will also inspire you and show you that it's possible.

Don't forget to consider your values and long-term goals. Earning extra money shouldn't mean compromising what's important to you. If you value spending time with your family, look for ways to earn money that don't require long hours away from home. If your long-term goal is to save up for a trip or a house, choose activities that will effectively help you achieve that goal.

Additionally, it's crucial to be realistic about your time and energy. We all have limitations, and it's important to recognize them. If you already have a full-time job, think about how much time you can realistically devote to a side hustle without burning yourself out. It's best to start small and gradually increase the time and effort you put into earning extra money. Remember, the key is to find a balance that allows you to enjoy life while increasing your income.

Last but not least, keep a positive and open attitude. Starting something new always comes with challenges, but also with many opportunities for learning and growth. Don't be discouraged if you don't see immediate results. Perseverance and patience are essential. Keep your mind open to new ideas and don't be afraid to make adjustments along the way. Over time, you'll find the best way to make extra money that aligns with who you are and what you love to do.

In short, knowing yourself is the crucial first step to making extra money in a way that is rewarding and sustainable. By understanding your passions, skills, and personality, and by considering your values and goals, you will be able to identify opportunities that will not only provide you with additional income, but also enrich your life. So take a moment to reflect on who you are and what you really want. This self-knowledge will guide you on the path to making extra money in a way that makes you happy and fulfilling.

Freelance and Consulting

Freelancing and consulting are two effective and flexible ways to earn extra money, especially if you already have a full-time job. These options allow you to leverage your skills and knowledge in your spare time, generating additional income without having to compromise your main job. Best of all, you can do it from the comfort of your home, at your own pace, and adapt it to your schedule.

Freelancing, also known as independent work, involves offering services to clients without being tied to a particular company. One of the biggest advantages of freelancing is the variety of fields you can work in. If you have skills in graphic design, writing, programming, digital marketing, translation, or even administrative tasks, there is a high demand for these services on platforms like Upwork, Freelancer, and Fiverr. To get started, you should first identify your strongest skills and create a profile on one or more of these platforms. Describe your services in detail, show examples of your previous work if possible, and set competitive prices. Don't be discouraged if you don't get many projects at first; with perseverance and good reviews from your first clients, your reputation will grow.

On the other hand, consulting is another great option for making extra money, especially if you have considerable experience in a specific field. As a consultant, you offer your knowledge and advice to companies or individuals who need help in areas in which you are an expert. This can be anything from business strategies, process improvements, technology advice, human resources, personal finances, to implementing new policies and practices. The first thing you should do is identify your area of expertise and then promote yourself through your professional network, social media such as LinkedIn, and your own website if you have one. It is useful to offer some initial consultations for free or at a reduced rate to attract your first clients and demonstrate your value.

Freelancing and consulting both have their own challenges. Competition can be high and it can sometimes be difficult to find clients, especially in the beginning. However, there are strategies you can use to stand out. Always keep your portfolio up to date, ask your satisfied clients to leave you positive reviews, and never underestimate the power of word-of-mouth recommendations. Also, keep training and updating yourself in your field; online courses and webinars are great resources to keep you up to date and improve your skills.

Organization and time management are essential when working as a freelancer or consultant, especially if you're balancing these projects with a full-time job. Set a clear schedule for your freelance or consulting tasks and try to be as disciplined as possible. Use project management tools like Trello or Asana to keep track of your tasks and deadlines. Also, make sure you communicate effectively with your clients; keep your clients updated on the progress of projects and be clear about delivery times and expectations.

In terms of income, freelancing and consulting can be very lucrative. Depending on your experience and the demand for your skills, you could earn anywhere from a few hundred to several thousand dollars a month. It's important to set fair rates that reflect your level of experience and the value you bring, but also to be competitive. Research how much other professionals in your field charge and adjust your rates accordingly. Don't be afraid to raise your prices as you gain more experience and build a solid reputation.

Finally, one of the great advantages of freelancing and consulting is the flexibility they offer. You can work from anywhere, as long as you have an internet connection and the necessary tools to do your job. This allows you to better manage your time and balance your work responsibilities with your personal life. Plus, as you develop your client base and build strong relationships, you can start receiving recurring work, which provides a more stable source of income.

In short, freelancing and consulting are great ways to make extra money using your skills and knowledge. They require dedication, organization, and a good dose of patience, but the rewards can be significant. By working on projects you are passionate about and helping others with your expertise, you will not only earn extra money, but you will also find great personal satisfaction. So, if you are looking for a flexible and effective way to increase your income, seriously consider freelancing or consulting.

Monetize Your Hobbies

Monetizing your hobbies is a fantastic way to earn extra money while enjoying what you love to do. Often times, our hobbies can seem like just recreational activities, but with a little creativity and effort, they can be transformed into lucrative sources of income. Whether you enjoy photography, cooking, gardening, writing, or any other activity, there are ways to turn these passions into money. This chapter will show you how to do it effectively and easily.

First, identify which of your hobbies have the potential to generate income. Make a list of all the activities you enjoy and are skilled at. Think about those that could be useful or entertaining to other people. For example, if you love baking, you could sell your products at local markets or online. If you enjoy photography, you could offer photo shoots or sell your photos through platforms like Shutterstock or Etsy. If you're good at painting, consider selling your work or even teaching art classes.

Once you've identified a hobby you want to monetize, research the market. Look at how other people are making money from similar activities. This will give you an idea of what's working and what's not. Search the internet, social media, and online communities to see examples and gather ideas. Also, research the prices others are charging for similar products or services so you can set your prices competitively.

The next step is to establish an online presence. Nowadays, having a digital presence is crucial for any type of business. Create profiles on popular social media sites like Instagram, Facebook, and Pinterest, where you can share your work and attract potential customers. If you sell products, consider opening an online store on platforms like Etsy, eBay, or Amazon Handmade. It's also helpful to have your own website where you can showcase your portfolio, offer information about your services, and allow customers to easily contact you.

To attract clients, you need to promote your work. Use social media to showcase what you do, share stories and behind-the-scenes footage to connect with your audience. Post regularly and use relevant hashtags to reach more people interested in your hobby. If you feel comfortable, consider making videos on YouTube or TikTok where you showcase your skills and offer tutorials. Not only will this attract clients, but it will also establish you as an expert in your field.

Another effective strategy is to participate in local markets, craft fairs, or community events where you can sell your products or promote your services. These events are great opportunities to connect face-to-face with potential clients and get direct feedback on your work. Additionally, carrying business cards and brochures can help people remember your business and contact you later.

Quality is key when monetizing a hobby. Make sure you offer high-quality products or services that will satisfy your customers. Not only will this help you make money, but it will also encourage word-of-mouth recommendations and positive online reviews, which are crucial to growing your business. Always look to improve and hone your skills. Take courses, read books, and stay on top of trends in your area to ensure you're offering the best.

It's important to manage your time well when monetizing a hobby, especially if you also have a full-time job. Set a schedule that allows you to dedicate enough time to your hobby without compromising your other responsibilities. Plan your days and weeks in advance, and set clear, achievable goals to stay focused and motivated. Use time management tools and productivity apps to help you stay on top of your tasks and deadlines.

Finally, stay passionate and enjoy the process. Monetizing a hobby can be an incredibly rewarding experience, but it can also be challenging. There will be times when things don't go your way, but don't be discouraged. Remember why you started in the first place: because you enjoy what you do. Keep that passion alive and allow it to drive you forward. Learn from your mistakes, celebrate your successes, and keep moving forward with determination.

In short, monetizing your hobbies is a great way to make extra money while doing what you love. Identify the right hobby, research the market, establish an online presence, promote your work, participate in local events, deliver quality, manage your time efficiently, and above all, stay passionate. With these steps, you can turn your hobby into a rewarding and sustainable source of income.

Teach What you Know

Teaching what you know is a wonderful way to earn extra money while helping others learn and grow. We all have knowledge and skills that we have acquired throughout our lives, whether through our education, work experiences, or hobbies. Sharing this knowledge with others is not only rewarding, but it can also be a lucrative source of income. In this chapter, we will explore how you can turn your skills and knowledge into profitable teaching opportunities.

First, identify what you are good at and what you could teach others. Think about your areas of expertise and the skills you have mastered. This can be anything from playing a musical instrument, cooking specific dishes, speaking a foreign language, to more technical skills like programming, graphic design, or accounting. The key is to choose something you are passionate about and feel comfortable teaching others.

Once you've identified your teaching area, decide how you want to share your knowledge. There are several ways to do this, depending on your preferences and the type of audience you want to reach. You can opt for in-person classes, online classes, workshops, seminars, one-on-one tutoring, or even creating online courses. Each format has its own advantages. In-person classes allow you to interact face-to-face with your students and offer a more personalized experience, while online classes and courses allow you to reach a wider audience and work from anywhere.

To start teaching, you'll need to prepare your teaching materials. This includes planning your lessons, creating presentations, study guides, practice exercises, and any other resources that can help your students learn effectively. Make sure your material is clear, organized, and easy to follow. If you're creating an online course, you'll also need to record your video lessons and edit the content to make it professional and engaging.

Promoting your classes is a crucial step in attracting students. Use social media to advertise your classes and share testimonials from past students. If you have a website, create a section dedicated to your teaching services, where people can find detailed information about your classes, read reviews, and get in touch with you. Platforms like YouTube, Facebook, Instagram, and LinkedIn are great for promoting your skills and reaching a wider audience. You can also consider paid advertising to reach more people interested in learning what you offer.

Another option to teach what you know is to join online teaching platforms like Udemy, Coursera, Skillshare, or Teachable. These platforms allow you to create and sell your courses to a global audience. Once your course is published, the platform takes care of promotion, student management, and payments, allowing you to focus on creating quality content. These platforms also often offer resources and guides to help you create successful courses.

Word of mouth is a powerful tool for attracting new students. Ask your current and former students to recommend your classes to their friends and family. Positive reviews and testimonials are crucial for building a good reputation and attracting more students. Make sure to ask for feedback after each class to find out what you are doing well and where you can improve.

Also, consider offering some free classes or webinars to attract new students. These free events allow people to try out your classes without commitment and can lead to paid enrollments. It's a great way to demonstrate your expertise and hook potential students.

The quality of your teaching is essential for long-term success. Make sure you are patient, understanding, and clear in your explanations. Adapt your teaching style to the needs and abilities of your students so that everyone can keep up and learn effectively. Stay up-to-date in your field and keep learning new techniques and knowledge that you can share with your students.

Finally, organize your time well to balance your classes with other responsibilities. Set a clear schedule and communicate it to your students. Use time management tools and calendars to keep track of your classes and make sure you meet your commitments. Good organization is key to providing a positive learning experience and keeping your students satisfied.

In short, teaching what you know is a rewarding and effective way to earn extra money. Identify your skills, choose the right teaching format, prepare your material, promote your classes, and offer quality teaching. With dedication and passion, you can turn your knowledge into a valuable source of income and make a difference in the lives of your students.

Small and Local Enterprises

Starting a small, local business can be a great way to make extra money while getting involved in your community. Local businesses have the advantage of allowing you to build close relationships with your customers, better understand their needs, and tailor your offering directly. Whether you want to open a small shop, offer services in your neighborhood, or create handmade products, local businesses can be very rewarding and lucrative. In this chapter, we'll explore how you can start and run a small, local business effectively.

First, it's important to identify a viable business idea that fits your skills and interests. Think about problems or needs you've noticed in your community. Maybe there's an unmet demand for certain products or services. For example, you could open a grocery store specializing in organic produce if you notice that options in your area are limited. Or perhaps you could offer landscaping services, appliance repair, or yoga classes if you have the necessary skills. The key is to find an idea that resonates with people in your area and plays to your strengths.

Once you have a clear idea, conduct market research to better understand your competition and potential customers. Visit similar businesses in your area, talk to the owners, and observe how they operate. Ask your friends, family, and neighbors what they think about your idea and whether they would be interested in your products or services. This information will help you refine your concept and ensure that there is a real demand for your business.

The next step is to create a solid business plan. A good business plan should include a detailed description of your idea, a market analysis, a marketing strategy, an operational plan, and financial projections. This document will serve as a roadmap and help you stay focused on your goals. Additionally, a well-crafted business plan is essential if you plan to seek outside funding, as banks and investors will want to see that you have thought carefully about every aspect of your venture.

Financing your business can be one of the biggest challenges when starting out. If you don't have enough capital of your own, consider the financing options available.

You can apply for a bank loan, look for local investors, or even launch a crowdfunding campaign. Additionally, some communities offer grants and support programs for small businesses. Research all the available options and choose the one that best suits your needs.

Once you have the funding, it's time to set up your business. This includes finding a suitable location if you're opening a brick-and-mortar store, or preparing your workspace if you're offering services from home. Make sure you comply with all local regulations, obtain the necessary licenses and permits, and set up an accounting system to keep your finances in order. Legality and organization are key to avoiding future problems and ensuring long-term success.

Promoting your business is crucial to attracting customers and generating sales. Use local marketing strategies such as distributing flyers, placing ads in local newspapers and magazines, and participating in fairs and community events. Social media can also be a powerful tool to reach your local audience. Create profiles on popular platforms and share regular content that showcases your products or services, tells your business story, and highlights positive customer reviews.

Customer service is a critical part of any local business. Make sure you treat every customer with kindness and respect, and respond quickly to their questions and needs. A good customer experience not only ensures repeat business, but also encourages positive word of mouth, which is essential to the growth of any small business.

To maintain and grow your business, it's important to be flexible and willing to adapt to your customers' changing needs. Listen to their feedback and adjust your offering as needed. Stay on top of trends in your industry and look for opportunities to innovate and improve. The ability to adapt quickly can be a significant advantage for small, local businesses.

Finally, enjoy the process of entrepreneurship. While it can be challenging and sometimes stressful, starting and running a small, local business can also be extremely rewarding. It gives you the opportunity to be your own boss, to create something you are truly passionate about, and to have a positive impact on your community.

In short, small and local businesses offer an excellent opportunity to earn extra money while connecting with your community. Identify a viable idea, conduct market research, create a business plan, secure financing, establish your business, promote your products or services, offer excellent customer service, and remain flexible and adaptable. With dedication and effort, your small business can thrive and become a significant source of additional income.

Collaborative Economy

The sharing economy has become a popular and effective way to earn extra money by leveraging resources you already have. This economic model is based on sharing goods and services with other people, allowing you to maximize their use and earn additional income. The sharing economy includes a wide range of activities, from renting out your home to tourists, to carpooling, to offering your skills for small tasks. In this chapter, we will explore the various ways you can participate in the sharing economy and how you can benefit from it.

One of the most well-known forms of the sharing economy is short-term property rentals through platforms like Airbnb. If you have a spare room in your house, an apartment you don't use, or even a vacation home, you can rent these spaces out to travelers. Not only does this allow you to earn extra money, but it also gives you the opportunity to meet new people from all over the world. To get started, simply sign up to a rental platform, take attractive photos of your space, set a competitive price, and post your listing. Make sure to keep your property clean and inviting to receive good reviews and attract more guests.

Another popular option is carpooling. Services like Uber and Lyft allow you to use your car to transport passengers and earn money in your spare time. If you already own a car and enjoy driving, this can be a great way to generate additional income. You just need to sign up as a driver, go through a verification process, and start accepting ride requests. In addition to earning money, carpooling also allows you to socialize and meet new people in your city.

If you prefer an option that doesn't require as much commitment, consider offering your skills and time for small tasks through platforms like TaskRabbit or Fiverr. TaskRabbit connects people who need help with everyday tasks, such as assembling furniture, making home repairs, or running errands, with people willing to do them. Fiverr, on the other hand, is a platform where you can offer online services, such as graphic design, writing, translation, and more. These platforms allow you to work flexibly and choose the tasks or projects that interest you the most.

Renting items is also a growing way to participate in the sharing economy. For example, if you have tools, sports equipment, or any other items that you don't use often, you can rent them out to people who need them temporarily. Platforms like Fat Llama make this type of exchange easy. Renting out your items not only allows you to earn extra money, but it also helps others access what they need without having to buy it new.

Sharing knowledge and skills through online teaching is another effective way to participate in the sharing economy. Platforms like Udemy and Coursera allow you to create and sell online courses on any topic you have expertise in. From cooking classes, photography, programming, to meditation techniques, there is a high demand for knowledge in a variety of areas. Creating an online course takes time and initial effort, but once it is published, it can generate passive income for a long time.

The collaborative economy also includes the concept of crowdfunding, where you can raise funds for your personal or business projects through platforms such as Kickstarter or Indiegogo. If you have an innovative idea for a product, an artistic project, or even a social cause, you can submit your proposal and receive financial support from people interested in your vision. Crowdfunding not only provides you with the funds necessary to carry out your project, but also connects you with a community of supporters and potential customers.

For those with culinary skills, the sharing economy offers opportunities to share your talents with others. Platforms like EatWith allow people to host dinner parties in their homes for guests looking for a unique dining experience. If you enjoy cooking and hosting people in your home, this can be a fun and lucrative way to make extra money.

The key to success in the sharing economy is trust and reputation. Sharing economy platforms often include review and rating systems that help build trust among users. Make sure you provide good service, are communicative, and follow through on your commitments to receive positive reviews. This will increase your visibility and attract more customers.

Participating in the sharing economy also requires an open mind and a willingness to try new things. Not every option will work for everyone, but experimenting with different platforms and services will help you find what best suits your skills and lifestyle. Plus, the sharing economy fosters a sense of community and cooperation, which can be very rewarding both personally and financially.

In short, the sharing economy offers numerous opportunities to make extra money using resources and skills you already possess. From renting out properties, sharing rides, offering services, renting items, teaching online, fundraising for projects, to sharing cooking skills, there are many ways to get involved. The key is to identify the opportunities that best fit your interests and skills, and offer good service to build a positive reputation. With a little creativity and effort, you can take advantage of the sharing economy to generate additional income and enrich your life.

Smart Investments

Investing wisely is one of the most effective ways to make your money work for you. Smart investments not only allow you to grow your wealth over time, but they also provide you with an additional source of income that can supplement your salary or even replace it in the future. In this chapter, we will explore different types of investments and how you can start investing strategically to maximize your returns.

One of the first things you need to understand about investing is the importance of diversification. Diversifying means not putting all of your money into one type of investment. By spreading your money across different assets, you reduce the risk of significant losses. For example, instead of investing all of your money in stocks from one company, you could invest in a variety of stocks from different sectors, bonds, and real estate. This strategy protects you against market volatility and provides you with greater financial stability.

Stocks are one of the most well-known and popular types of investments. When you buy stocks, you are buying a small piece of a company. If the company is successful and its value increases, the value of your shares will also increase. However, if the company is struggling and its value decreases, the value of your shares will decrease. It is important to do your research and choose companies with a strong track record and growth prospects. Additionally, you may want to consider investing in index funds or mutual funds, which pool together many different stocks and allow for automatic diversification.

Bonds are another investment option that can offer more stable income. When you buy a bond, you are lending money to a company or government in exchange for regular interest payments. Bonds are typically less volatile than stocks, making them an attractive option for investors looking for stability. There are different types of bonds, such as Treasury bonds, corporate bonds, and municipal bonds, each with different levels of risk and return. It is important to understand the terms and conditions of each bond before investing.

The real estate market also offers interesting opportunities for smart investments. Buying properties to rent can generate consistent passive income through rental payments. Plus, properties can increase in value over time, allowing you to make a profit when you decide to sell them. However, investing in real estate requires a significant upfront investment and time to manage the properties. You should also consider maintenance costs and possible periods without tenants. Researching the local real estate market and working with professionals can help you make informed decisions.

Investments in mutual funds are an attractive option for those who prefer a more hands-on approach. A mutual fund pools money from many investors to purchase a diversified portfolio of assets. This can include stocks, bonds, real estate, and other financial instruments. Mutual funds are managed by professionals who make investment decisions on your behalf, allowing you to benefit from their expertise. There are different types of funds, such as equity funds, fixed-income funds, and balanced funds, each with different objectives and risk levels.

Cryptocurrency investing has gained popularity in recent years. Cryptocurrencies like Bitcoin and Ethereum are digital currencies that use blockchain technology to secure transactions. While cryptocurrencies can offer significant returns, they are also extremely volatile and risky. If you decide to invest in cryptocurrencies, it is crucial to do thorough research and only invest money that you are willing to lose. It is also important to keep your cryptocurrencies safe by using reliable digital wallets.

Another form of investment that is gaining ground is real estate and business crowdfunding. Through crowdfunding platforms, you can invest small amounts of money in real estate projects or startups. This allows you to diversify your portfolio with a lower initial investment and access opportunities that would otherwise be out of reach. However, these investments also carry risks and it is important to research each project and platform before committing your money.

Investing in education and personal development is an investment in yourself that can offer significant returns over the long term. By acquiring new skills and knowledge, you increase your value in the job market and your chances of earning more money. This can include earning an advanced degree, attending workshops and seminars, or learning new technical skills. Investing in your education can also open up new business and entrepreneurial opportunities for you.

A smart investment strategy also involves planning for the future and setting clear financial goals. Define your investment goals, such as saving for retirement, buying a home, or funding your children's education. Then, develop an investment plan that will help you achieve these goals. It's important to review and adjust your plan regularly to ensure you're staying on track and adapt to changes in the market and your personal situation.

Finally, working with a financial advisor can be very beneficial, especially if you are new to the world of investing. A financial advisor can help you assess your goals, risk tolerance, and financial situation to develop a personalized investment strategy. They can provide you with insight and guidance to make informed decisions and avoid common mistakes.

In short, smart investing involves diversifying your investments, researching and understanding different types of assets, and planning for the future. Whether you invest in stocks, bonds, real estate, mutual funds, cryptocurrencies, crowdfunding, or your own education, it's important to make informed, strategic decisions. Over time, smart investments can help you generate additional income, grow your wealth, and achieve your financial goals.

Online Product Sales

Selling products online is one of the most effective and accessible ways to make extra money. With the growth of e-commerce, more and more people are taking advantage of the opportunity to sell products online. Whether you have a talent for creating crafts, clothing, jewelry, or simply want to resell products you bought at a good price, the online marketplace offers you a platform to reach a global audience. In this chapter, we'll explore the steps necessary to start selling products online and how to maximize your earnings.

The first step to selling products online is deciding what you want to sell. This can be something you already do as a hobby, such as knitting scarves or making handmade candles, or it can be something you buy in bulk to resell. It's important to choose a product that you're passionate about and that you think will be in demand in the market. Researching which products are popular and which are in high demand can help you make an informed decision. You can use tools like Google Trends, Amazon Best Sellers, or even research on social media to identify trends and market needs.

Once you've decided what product to sell, the next step is to set up your online store. There are several e-commerce platforms you can use to create your store, such as Etsy, eBay, Amazon, or Shopify. Each of these platforms has its own advantages and disadvantages, so it's important to research which one best suits your needs. Etsy, for example, is ideal for handmade products and vintage items, while Amazon is perfect for new and high-demand products. Shopify, on the other hand, allows you to create a custom store and run your own website.

After choosing your platform, it's time to set up your store. This includes creating a catchy, memorable name, designing a logo that represents your brand, and writing detailed, engaging descriptions for each of your products. Make sure to take high-quality photos that clearly show your products from different angles. Photos should be clear, well-lit, and professional, as low-quality images can deter potential buyers. Additionally, descriptions should be detailed and highlight the features and benefits of your products.

Once your store is set up, the next step is to set prices for your products. It's important to strike a balance between being competitive and making sure you make a profit. Research how much other sellers are charging for similar products and adjust your prices accordingly. Don't forget to consider production costs, shipping, and the fees of the platform you're selling on. Offering occasional promotions or discounts can attract more customers and increase your sales.

Marketing is a crucial part of being successful at selling products online. Use social media to promote your store and reach a wider audience. Platforms like Instagram, Facebook, and Pinterest are great for showcasing your products and attracting followers. Regularly post engaging content, such as photos of your products, demo videos, and testimonials from satisfied customers. You can also use paid social media ads to reach a more targeted audience. Collaborating with influencers and bloggers in your niche can also be an effective strategy to increase your store's visibility.

Another effective marketing strategy is email marketing. Collect emails from your customers and send them regular newsletters with updates on new products, special offers, and news from your store. Maintaining constant communication with your customers can help build a strong relationship and foster loyalty. Additionally, offering excellent customer service is critical to your store's success. Respond quickly to customer questions and comments, and be sure to resolve any issues efficiently and professionally.

Inventory management and shipping are key aspects that you need to handle carefully. Keep an up-to-date record of your inventory to avoid selling products you don't have in stock. Also, choose a shipping method that is fast and reliable. Offering free or cheap shipping options can attract more customers and increase your sales. It's also important to package your products safely to ensure they reach buyers in perfect condition. Consider using sustainable packaging materials to reduce your environmental impact and attract environmentally conscious consumers.

Analyzing your sales and customer behavior is essential to optimizing your online sales strategy. Use the analytics tools offered by e-commerce platforms to gain insights into which products are most popular, which promotions are most effective, and how customers interact with your store. This information will allow you to make informed decisions and adjust your strategy to maximize your profits. Experiment with different product types, prices, and marketing strategies to see what works best for your store.

Finally, staying up to date with market trends and being willing to adapt is crucial to long-term success in selling products online. E-commerce is constantly evolving, and what works today may not be effective tomorrow. Keep learning and improving your marketing and sales skills, and don't be afraid to try new things. Participate in online seller communities and forums to share experiences and learn from others. Flexibility and a willingness to adapt will help you keep your store relevant and competitive in the market.

In short, selling products online is a great way to make extra money and can become a significant source of income if done correctly. By choosing products you are passionate about, setting up an attractive store, setting competitive prices, and using effective marketing strategies, you can create a successful and sustainable business. The key is to be persistent, willing to learn and adapt, and always keep a focus on providing excellent customer service. With the right time and effort, you can transform your online store into a thriving and rewarding source of income.

Affiliate Marketing

Affiliate marketing is an effective and accessible way to earn extra money, especially if you already have a job. This method allows you to generate income by promoting other companies' products or services and earning a commission for each sale or action that is made through your recommendations. In this chapter, we will explore in detail how affiliate marketing works, how you can get started, and what strategies you can use to maximize your earnings.

Affiliate marketing works in a simple way. Companies that want to increase their sales or subscribers offer affiliate programs that you can sign up for for free. Once you sign up, you get a unique affiliate link that you can share on your blog, social media, email, or any other communication channel you use. Every time someone clicks on your link and makes a purchase or completes a specific action, you earn a commission. The amount of the commission varies by company and product, but can range from a few percent to 50 percent or more of the sales price.

To get started in affiliate marketing, the first step is to identify a niche or area of interest that you feel comfortable and have some knowledge in. This can be anything you are passionate about, such as technology, fashion, health, fitness, or even specific hobbies like gardening or video games. Choosing a niche will help you focus your efforts and attract a specific audience that will trust your recommendations.

Once you have chosen your niche, the next step is to find suitable affiliate programs. You can start by looking at popular affiliate marketing platforms such as Amazon Associates, ShareASale, ClickBank, and Commission Junction. These platforms offer a wide variety of products and services that you can promote. Additionally, many companies have their own affiliate programs, so you can also visit the websites of your favorite brands and look for the affiliate section.

After signing up for affiliate programs, it's important to create quality content that will engage your audience and motivate them to click on your affiliate links. If you have a blog, write detailed reviews, product comparisons, buying guides, and informative articles that are helpful and relevant to your readers. If you prefer social media, create engaging posts, videos, stories, and live content where you can talk about the products and show how you use them in your daily life. The key is to be honest and authentic in your recommendations, as your audience's trust is critical to success in affiliate marketing.

In addition to creating content, it's important to optimize your marketing strategies to increase the visibility of your affiliate links. Use search engine optimization (SEO) techniques to improve your blog's ranking in Google search results. This includes using relevant keywords, creating catchy titles, and optimizing your images and links. You can also use email marketing to keep your audience informed about new products and special offers. Send out regular newsletters with valuable content and make sure to include your affiliate links in the right places.

Another effective strategy is to participate in online communities and forums related to your niche. Share your knowledge and experiences, answer questions, and provide useful links that include your affiliate links. Actively participating in these communities can help you build your reputation and attract more people to your content. However, it's important not to be too aggressive in promoting your links, as this can backfire. Instead, focus on providing value and helping others.

Social media is also a powerful tool for affiliate marketing. Create profiles on platforms like Instagram, Facebook, Twitter, and Pinterest, and share content related to your affiliate products. Use relevant hashtags to increase the visibility of your posts and attract a wider audience. Consider collaborating with influencers or bloggers in your niche to expand your reach and attract new followers. Collaborations can include sponsored posts, giveaways, or mentions on their media channels.

Analytics and optimization are crucial components of affiliate marketing. Use the analytics tools provided by affiliate platforms to monitor the performance of your links. Pay attention to metrics like the number of clicks, conversions, and commissions generated. This will help you identify which strategies are working and which need tweaking. Experiment with different types of content, link placements, and promotion tactics to see what yields the best results. Continuous improvement is essential to maximizing your affiliate marketing earnings.

Finally, it is important to have patience and persistence. Affiliate marketing does not generate significant income overnight. It requires time, effort, and consistency to build an audience and gain their trust. Don't get discouraged if you don't see immediate results. Keep creating quality content, optimizing your strategies, and learning from your experiences. Over time, your dedication will pay off and you will be able to enjoy the benefits of earning extra money through affiliate marketing.

In short, affiliate marketing is a great way to generate extra income while working on something you are passionate about. By choosing a niche, joining affiliate programs, creating valuable content, optimizing your marketing strategies, and being persistent, you can build a sustainable and rewarding source of income. Remember that the key to success is authenticity and trust from your audience. With dedication and effort, you can transform affiliate marketing into an integral part of your strategy to earn extra money.

Content Creation

Content creation is a great way to generate additional income while doing something you are passionate about. In the digital age, content is king, and there are many ways you can leverage your skills and knowledge to create content that will attract an audience and allow you to monetize your efforts. This chapter will focus on how you can get started creating content, the different platforms available, and strategies to maximize your income.

First, it's important to identify what type of content you'd like to create. This largely depends on your interests and skills. Content can take many forms, such as writing blogs, recording videos, producing podcasts, taking photographs, creating digital art, and more. Think about what you're passionate about and good at, and choose a format that allows you to best express yourself. For example, if you enjoy writing, a blog may be a great option. If you prefer to talk and have a pleasant voice, a podcast might be the way to go. If you enjoy being in front of a camera, consider creating a YouTube channel.

Once you've decided on the type of content you want to create, it's time to choose the right platform. There are many options available, and each has its own advantages. If you decide to blog, platforms like WordPress, Blogger, or Medium are very popular and easy to use. For videos, YouTube and TikTok are great options due to their large audiences and the tools they offer for creators. If you prefer podcasts, platforms like Anchor, Spotify, and Apple Podcasts are ideal for distributing your content. You can also consider Instagram or Pinterest if your focus is more visual and relies on photography or digital art.

The next step is to create high-quality content that resonates with your audience. This means you need to research and understand your target audience. What type of content are they interested in? What problems or questions do they have that you can help solve? Use this information to create content that is useful, informative, and entertaining. For example, if you decide to create a gardening blog, you could write guides on how to plant different types of flowers, tips for caring for plants, and reviews of gardening tools.

If you make videos about cooking, you could share recipes, cooking hacks, and step-by-step demonstrations.

Consistency is key when it comes to content creation. It's important to set a publishing schedule and stick to it. Not only does this help you stay organized, but it also sets expectations for your audience. If you post content on a regular basis, your followers will know when to expect new material and will be more inclined to come back. This also helps build your personal brand and online presence.

Once you've started creating and publishing content, it's time to think about how to monetize your efforts. There are several ways to make money through content creation. One of the most common is through advertising. If you have a blog, you can join programs like Google AdSense to display ads on your website. Every time someone clicks on one of the ads, you earn a small commission. If you make videos on YouTube, you can join the YouTube Partner Program and earn money from ads that are displayed before, during, or after your videos.

Another way to monetize your content is through affiliate marketing. This involves promoting other companies' products or services and earning a commission for every sale that is made through your affiliate links. For example, if you write a tech blog, you can include links to products on Amazon and earn a commission every time someone purchases through your link. Many companies and brands have affiliate programs, so be sure to do your research and join those that are relevant to your content.

Sponsorship is another potential revenue stream. As your audience grows, brands may be interested in sponsoring your content. This can include creating sponsored content, where you mention or recommend specific products or services, or including sponsored mentions in your videos or podcasts. It's important to be transparent with your audience about any sponsorship and make sure the brands you work with align with your values and the interests of your audience.

Selling products or services is also a viable option. If you have specialized skills or knowledge, you can create and sell your own digital products, such as eBooks, online courses, templates, or graphics. If you are an artist, you can sell your artwork or prints. You can also offer services, such as consulting, tutoring, or graphic design. Not only does this allow you to make money, but it also helps you establish yourself as an expert in your field.

Finally, it is important to promote your content to reach a wider audience. Use social media to share your posts, interact with your audience, and collaborate with other creators. Participate in online communities related to your niche and share your content there. Promotion is essential to attract new followers and build a loyal audience.

In short, content creation is a great way to make extra money while doing something you are passionate about. By identifying your niche, choosing the right platform, creating high-quality and consistent content, and exploring various forms of monetization, you can turn your passion into an additional source of income. Remember that success in content creation takes time and effort, but with dedication and creativity, you can achieve it.

Surveys and Product Testing

Taking surveys and product testing is an easy and accessible way to earn extra money in your spare time. This option is especially good for those looking for additional income without having to make a large investment of time or money. In this chapter, I will explain how you can start earning money by taking surveys and testing products, where to find these opportunities, and some tips to maximize your earnings.

First, it's important to understand how paid surveys and product testing work. Market research companies and product manufacturers are interested in getting consumer feedback to improve their products and services. To do this, they hire survey and product testing companies that recruit people like you to participate. In exchange for your time and opinions, they pay you in cash, gift cards, or free products.

To start making money with surveys, the first step is to sign up for several paid survey websites. There are many options available, and some of the most popular ones include Swagbucks, Toluna, Pinecone Research, and Survey Junkie. It is advisable to sign up for multiple sites to have access to a larger number of surveys and thus increase your chances of making money. During registration, you will be asked to fill out a profile with basic information about yourself, such as your age, gender, location, and spending habits. This information is used to match you with surveys that are relevant to you.

Once you've registered and completed your profile, you'll start receiving invitations to take surveys. Surveys can range in length and pay, from short five-minute surveys that pay one dollar, to longer thirty-minute surveys that pay five dollars or more. It's important to complete surveys honestly and accurately, as research companies value the quality of responses. Additionally, many platforms have systems in place to detect inconsistent or random responses, which could result in disqualification from future surveys.

In addition to surveys, product testing is another great way to make extra money. As with surveys, you sign up for websites that offer opportunities to test products. Some well-known sites include Vindale Research,

UserTesting, and Product Report Card. After you sign up, they will send products to your home for you to test and then provide feedback on. These products can range from food and drink to beauty products and electronics. In exchange for your detailed feedback, you can get paid in cash, gift cards, or even keep the products you test.

One of the benefits of product testing is that you often get to try out the latest releases before the general public, which can be a fun and exciting experience. Plus, product testing often pays more than surveys, especially if the product is expensive or requires detailed testing. For example, testing a new tech gadget can pay you fifty dollars or more, plus allow you to keep the product.

To maximize your earnings from surveys and product testing, here are some helpful tips. First, try to set aside a specific time each day or week to complete surveys and tests. Consistency is key to racking up extra income. Second, make sure to complete your profile on each survey website and keep it updated. This will increase your chances of receiving relevant surveys and tests. Third, be honest and detailed in your answers. Companies value quality feedback, and you're more likely to be invited to participate in future studies if you provide helpful feedback. Fourth, look for websites and apps that offer bonuses for signing up or referring friends. These bonuses can boost your initial earnings.

While surveys and product testing won't make you rich, they can provide a steady stream of extra income with relatively little effort. It's an especially attractive option for those who have downtime during the day, such as during lunch, on public transportation, or while watching TV. Plus, it's a flexible way to make money, as you can do it from anywhere and at any time you have available.

In short, earning extra money by participating in surveys and product testing is an accessible and convenient way to increase your income. By registering on various websites, completing your profile, and being consistent and honest in your answers, you can take advantage of this opportunity to earn cash rewards, gift cards, and free products. It doesn't require a significant investment of time or money, making it a great option for anyone looking for extra income without compromising their core responsibilities.

Rewards Apps and Websites

In today's world, rewards apps and websites have become a popular and accessible way to earn some extra money. These platforms pay you for doing simple tasks like watching videos, answering surveys, shopping online, or even just walking around. In this chapter, we'll explore how these apps and websites work, what some of the best options available are, and how you can maximize your earnings using these tools.

Rewards apps and websites operate on a very simple principle: they reward you for completing activities that you probably already do in your daily life. For example, there are apps that pay you for shopping at your favorite stores, and others that reward you for staying active and walking a certain number of steps each day. The key to getting the most out of these platforms is to understand how they work and find the ones that best fit your habits and preferences.

One of the most well-known rewards apps is Swagbucks. Swagbucks pays you for completing a variety of tasks, including watching videos, answering surveys, playing games, and making online purchases through their portal. Each time you complete one of these tasks, you earn points called Swagbucks, which you can then redeem for gift cards or cash through PayPal. Swagbucks is easy to use and has a wide variety of tasks, making it a versatile option for those looking to earn a little extra money in their spare time.

Another popular app is Rakuten, formerly known as Ebates. Rakuten gives you back a percentage of the money you spend on online purchases in the form of cashback. All you have to do is sign up for Rakuten, find your favorite store through their portal, and make your purchase as usual. Rakuten works with a wide variety of retailers, from clothing stores to travel sites, so there's a good chance you can earn cashback on your regular purchases. At the end of each quarter, Rakuten sends you a check or deposits the cashback into your PayPal account, making it an easy way to save money on purchases you were already planning to make.

If you love walking and would like to earn money for staying active, Sweatcoin is a great option. Sweatcoin is an app that pays you to walk. Every time you reach a certain number of steps, you earn Sweatcoins, which you can redeem for rewards like products, services, or even cash. The app uses your phone's GPS to track your steps and make sure you're actually walking. Not only does Sweatcoin motivate you to stay fit, but it also allows you to earn rewards for doing so.

InboxDollars is another rewards website that pays you for doing simple tasks like reading emails, answering surveys, playing games, and watching videos. Like Swagbucks, InboxDollars pays you cash or gift cards for completing these activities. One of the great things about InboxDollars is that it offers a welcome bonus when you sign up, giving you an initial boost in your earnings. Plus, it's easy to use and offers a variety of ways to earn money, making it attractive for those looking to diversify their extra income streams.

For those who enjoy trying out new products and sharing their opinions, Vindale Research is a great option. Vindale Research pays you for completing opinion surveys and product testing. Unlike some other survey sites, Vindale pays in cash rather than points, which may be more appealing to those who prefer direct monetary rewards. Additionally, surveys on Vindale tend to be more detailed and therefore may pay more than surveys on other sites.

To maximize your earnings using rewards apps and websites, here are some practical tips. First, sign up for multiple platforms to diversify your income streams and increase your earning opportunities. By doing so, you'll be able to take advantage of the different tasks and rewards each platform offers. Second, set up a regular schedule to complete tasks on these apps. Spending a few minutes each day watching videos, answering surveys, or making purchases through a cashback portal can add up over time. Third, take advantage of welcome bonuses and special promotions that many of these platforms offer. These bonuses can give you a nice jumpstart and help you reach the payout threshold more quickly.

Also, make sure to keep your profiles on these apps and websites up to date. Filling out your profile with accurate and detailed information can increase your chances of receiving relevant surveys and offers. Finally, review the redemption options available on each platform and choose those that best fit your needs and preferences. Some people prefer to receive gift cards to their favorite stores, while others prefer to receive cash via PayPal.

In short, rewards apps and websites are an accessible and flexible way to earn extra money in your spare time. By signing up to various platforms, establishing a regular routine, and taking advantage of bonuses and promotions, you can maximize your earnings and enjoy the rewards these tools offer. Whether you love shopping online, walking, or just spending a few minutes a day doing simple tasks, there's a rewards app or website that suits you.

Temporary and Seasonal Jobs

Temporary and seasonal jobs are a great way to make extra money without committing to long-term employment. These jobs are especially useful if you have a flexible schedule or availability during certain times of the year. Additionally, seasonal jobs are often related to holidays, special events, or specific periods of the year, making them unique and often quite entertaining. In this chapter, we'll explore what temporary and seasonal jobs are, how to find them, and some specific examples of these types of employment.

First, let's understand what temporary jobs are. A temporary job is one that lasts for a limited duration, from a few weeks to several months. These jobs are ideal for people looking for extra income without a long-term commitment. On the other hand, seasonal jobs are those that are concentrated during certain times of the year, such as the holiday season, summer, or fall harvests. Both types of jobs can offer a variety of opportunities in different industries, from retail to agriculture.

To find temporary and seasonal jobs, you can use several strategies. One of the most effective ways is to search online at job websites that specialize in short-term work. Sites like Indeed, Glassdoor, and LinkedIn often have sections dedicated to temporary and seasonal jobs. You can also visit companies' websites directly, as many post temporary employment opportunities on their sites. Another option is to sign up with temporary staffing agencies, which are responsible for matching workers with employers who need staff for a specific period of time.

Once you've identified some temporary or seasonal job opportunities, it's important to adequately prepare for the application process. Make sure you have an up-to-date resume that highlights your relevant skills and experiences. If the seasonal job requires specific skills, such as retail sales knowledge during the holiday season, be sure to highlight those on your resume. Additionally, being willing to work flexible hours or weekends can increase your chances of being hired, as many seasonal jobs require availability at non-traditional hours.

Now, let's look at some specific examples of temporary and seasonal jobs. During the holiday season, many retail stores and malls need additional staff to handle the increase in customers. These jobs can include cashier, shelf stocker, gift wrapper, and sales assistant positions. The advantage of these jobs is that they often offer flexible hours, making them perfect for those looking to supplement their income without leaving their main job.

Another common example of seasonal work is in the hospitality industry during the summer. Hotels, resorts, and restaurants in tourist destinations often need more staff during the summer months to serve tourists. These jobs can include roles such as waiter, receptionist, housekeeping staff, and lifeguard. Additionally, working in a tourist environment can be a fun and rewarding experience, allowing you to meet people from different places and enjoy a dynamic atmosphere.

Farming also offers many seasonal job opportunities, especially during harvest times. Depending on the region and type of crop, you might find jobs picking fruits, vegetables, or flowers. These jobs are often physically demanding, but they can offer good wages and the opportunity to work outdoors. Additionally, some employers offer accommodation and meals, which can be an added bonus.

Special events and festivals also create a high demand for temporary workers. For example, music festivals, fairs, and expos need staff for tasks such as ticket sales, stage set-up, food and beverage service, and security. Working at these events can be an exciting experience and a great way to earn extra money in a short period of time.

Temporary office jobs are also common, especially during periods of high demand, such as fiscal year-end or during large projects. These jobs can include roles such as administrative assistant, temporary accountant, or technical support. If you have specific skills in areas such as accounting, information technology, or administration, these jobs can offer you a good opportunity to earn extra money while developing your professional skills.

Finally, let's not forget temporary jobs related to back-to-school. Before the start of the school year, many school supply stores, bookstores, and department stores are looking for additional staff to handle the increase in sales. These jobs can include roles such as sales assistant, cashier, and inventory staff. If you have availability during the end of summer, these jobs can be a great way to make extra money right before the new school year starts.

In short, temporary and seasonal jobs offer a variety of opportunities to make extra money without making a long-term commitment. Whether you're interested in working in retail during the holidays, hospitality during the summer, farming during harvest, special events, offices during peak periods, or retail during back-to-school, there are plenty of options available. The key is to be prepared, flexible, and actively seek out these opportunities. With a little effort and planning, temporary and seasonal jobs can be an effective and fun way to supplement your income.

Work-Life Balance and Extra Income

Finding a balance between work, personal life, and generating extra income can seem like a difficult task, but it is essential to maintaining mental health and overall well-being. The key is to be well-organized, set clear priorities, and find ways to integrate extra activities without sacrificing quality of life. In this chapter, we will explore how to achieve this balance effectively, providing specific and direct tips that will help you manage your work and personal responsibilities while generating extra income.

First, it's important to recognize that time is a limited resource. We all have the same twenty-four hours in a day, so time management is essential. A good way to start is to make a list of all your daily responsibilities and activities. This includes your main job, household chores, time with family and friends, and any other activities that are part of your daily routine. Once you have this list, identify areas where you can be more efficient or where you can reduce the time spent without affecting the quality of your activities.

Once you have a clear idea of how you are spending your time, the next step is to prioritize your activities. Not all tasks are of equal importance, so it is essential to identify which ones are the most critical and which ones can wait. This will allow you to free up time to spend on activities that generate extra income. For example, if you find that you spend a lot of time watching television or browsing social media, consider reducing this time and using it for something more productive.

Now that you've identified and prioritized your activities, it's time to set up a schedule that allows you to effectively integrate your efforts to generate extra income without sacrificing your personal time. Creating a schedule will not only help you stay organized, but it will also allow you to realistically see how much time you can dedicate to additional activities. It's important to be honest with yourself about your capabilities and limits. If you try to spread yourself too thin, you could end up feeling overwhelmed and stressed, which would impact both your main job and your personal life.

A crucial aspect of work-life balance is learning to say no. It can be tempting to accept every opportunity that comes along to earn extra money, but it's critical to recognize your limits. Taking on too many responsibilities can lead to burnout, which in turn will affect your performance in all areas of your life. Evaluate each extra income opportunity based on its impact on your time and overall well-being. If an opportunity seems too demanding, consider looking for more manageable alternatives or adjusting your expectations.

Another helpful tip is to take advantage of available technologies and tools to make your extra income-generating activities more efficient. For example, if you decide to sell products online, use platforms that make inventory management and the sales process easier. If you opt for freelance work, use project management and communication apps that help you stay organized and in touch with your clients. These tools can save time and reduce stress, allowing you to focus on the tasks that really matter.

It's also essential to make time to look after your health and wellbeing. Work-life balance isn't just about managing your time effectively, but also about making sure you're taking care of your body and mind. Make sure you build time into your schedule for exercise, rest and activities you enjoy. Regular exercise not only improves your physical health, but it can also reduce stress and boost your mood. Likewise, adequate rest is crucial to maintaining a high level of energy and productivity.

Involving family and friends in your extra income-generating activities can be another effective way to maintain balance. If you have an online sales venture, consider involving your family in the process. Not only will it help you manage your time better, but it can also be a great way to spend time together and strengthen family ties. Similarly, sharing your goals and progress with close friends can provide you with an additional support system and motivation.

Finally, it's important to regularly review and adjust your schedule and priorities.

Life changes and so will your needs and circumstances. Review your progress regularly and adjust your plans as needed. Keep an open and flexible mind to adapt to new opportunities and challenges. Remember that perfect balance is not static, but a continuous process of adjustments and improvements.

In conclusion, finding a balance between work, personal life and generating extra income requires organization, prioritization and good time management. By setting a realistic schedule, learning to say no, using technological tools, taking care of your health and well-being, and involving your loved ones in your activities, you can achieve this balance and enjoy a more productive and fulfilling life. With a conscious and planned approach, it is possible to integrate extra income-generating activities without sacrificing your quality of life.

Inspiration and Success Stories

Inspiration is a powerful tool when we are looking to generate extra income. Hearing success stories from ordinary people who have achieved great things can give us the drive and motivation to keep going. In this chapter, we will explore several success stories that demonstrate how it is possible to transform a simple idea into a significant source of additional income. These stories will show us that with dedication, creativity, and perseverance, anyone can achieve their financial goals.

Let's start with the story of Ana, a mother of two who had always had a passion for cooking. Ana used to make desserts for her family and friends, who constantly praised her culinary skills. One day, a friend suggested that she start selling her desserts online. Ana was skeptical at first, but decided to give it a try. She created a social media page and started posting photos of her creations. To her surprise, orders started coming in quickly. In no time, Ana managed to establish a home-based baking business, generating significant extra income that allowed her to contribute to the family budget and save up for her dream vacation.

Another inspiring story is that of Juan, a young man who is passionate about photography. Juan worked full-time in an office, but always carried his camera everywhere, capturing special moments. His friends and family often asked him to take photos at events and celebrations. One day, a friend suggested that he offer his services as a freelance photographer. Juan created an online portfolio and began promoting his services in his spare time. At first, his clients were mainly acquaintances, but over time, his reputation grew and he began receiving requests from strangers. Today, Juan works fewer hours at his main job and devotes more time to his passion for photography, which has allowed him to have a more balanced and fulfilling life.

There's also the case of Laura, a graphic designer who had always had a knack for drawing. Laura decided to open an online store to sell her illustrations and designs on products like t-shirts, mugs, and notebooks. She used e-commerce platforms that facilitate print-on-demand, which meant she didn't need to invest in large amounts of inventory. Through social media and digital marketing, Laura managed to attract a sizable audience. Her online store not only provided her with extra income, but also gave her the opportunity to work on creative projects and develop her own artistic style.

Another inspiring example is Carlos, who had a deep knowledge of bicycle repair. During the weekends, Carlos used to help his friends fix their bikes for free. One day, a friend suggested that he offer his services to the public. Carlos set up a small workshop in his garage and began advertising his services in his neighborhood. Demand was high, and soon Carlos found himself working on bikes all over the city. His reputation for providing quality service at a fair price allowed him to expand his business. Today, Carlos has turned his passion into a steady source of income, and he has been able to reduce his hours at his main job to dedicate more time to his workshop.

Finally, we have the story of Marta, an English teacher who had always enjoyed teaching. Marta decided to start tutoring online for students who wanted to improve their English. Using video conferencing platforms and social media marketing, Marta was able to build a solid base of students. As her reputation grew, so did her client list. Marta found that tutoring not only provided her with extra income, but also allowed her to connect with people around the world and do what she was most passionate about.

These success stories share several common elements: they all found ways to monetize their passions and skills, started small, and used technology to reach a wider audience. Furthermore, they all demonstrated dedication and perseverance, which allowed them to overcome initial challenges and build successful businesses. Their experiences teach us that no matter how busy we are with our daily responsibilities, there are always opportunities to explore and leverage our skills and passions to generate additional income.

If you're looking for inspiration to start your own journey toward generating extra income, these stories can serve as powerful examples of what's possible. Think about what you're passionate about, the skills you have, and how you could share them with others. With creativity, effort, and a willingness to learn and adapt, you too can create your own success story. It's not just about making money, it's about finding ways to do what you love and improve your quality of life in the process.

www.ingramcontent.com/pod-product-compliance
Lightning Source LLC
LaVergne TN
LVHW040944150826
845672LV00002B/530

* 9 7 9 8 2 2 7 9 7 8 9 4 3 *